ROADSIGNS

Spirituality and Homily Ideas for the Weekdays of Lent

JAY CORMIER

Resource Publications, Inc.
160 East Virginia Street, Suite 290
San Jose, CA 95112

Editorial Director: Kenneth Guentert
Production Editor: Elizabeth J. Asborno
Cover Design: Ben Lizardi
Cover Production: Ron Niewald
Production Assistant: Allison Cunningham

Library of Congress Cataloging-in-Publication Data

Cormier, Jay.
  Roadsigns: spirituality for the weekdays of Lent.
    1. Lent—Prayer-books and devotions—English.
  2. Catholic Church—Prayer-books and devotions—English.
  I. Title.
  BX2170.L4C64 1987 242'.34 87-62534
  ISBN: 0-89390-107-5

5 4 3 2 1

Grateful acknowledgment is made for permission to reprint excerpts from the following copyrighted material:

Selections in Act 1, scene 12, and Act II, scene 17 from *Amadeus* by Peter Hall. Copyright © 1980, 1981. Reprinted by permission of Harper & Row, Publishers, Inc.; "Pope Meets in Jail With His Attacker" by Henry Kamm, *The New York Times*, December 28, 1983. Copyright © 1983 by The New York Times Company. Reprinted by permission; Editorial: "As Brothers," *The New York Times*, December 29, 1983. Copyright © 1983 by The New York Times Company. Reprinted by permission; "*I TOUCH THE FUTURE ... ": The Story of Christa McAuliffe* by Robert T. Hohler. Copyright © 1986 by Robert T. Hohler. Reprinted by permission of Random House, Inc.; "Ethics in Business: Answers by a Values Consultant to Top Companies" by Thomas C. Hayes, *The New York Times*, October 12, 1986. Copyright © 1986 by The New York Times Company. Reprinted by permission; "Messenger for the ten thousandth" by Harry James Cargas, *Commonweal* Magazine, October 24, 1986. Copyright © 1986 by *Commonweal* Foundation, 15 Dutch Street, New York, N.Y., 10038 (subscriptions: $28 per year). Reprinted by permission; *Heading Home* by Paul Tsongas. Copyright © 1984 by Paul Tsongas. Reprinted by permission by Alfred A. Knopf, Inc.; *When All You've Ever Wanted Isn't Enough* by Rabbi Harold Kushner. Copyright © 1986 by Kushner Enterprises, Inc. Reprinted by permission by Simon and Schuster, Inc.; "Dr. Dooley Changed Their Lives," by Catharine A. Lee, *St. Anthony Messenger*, March 1987. Copyright © 1987 by the St. Anthony Messenger Press, 1615 Republic Street, Cincinnati, Ohio 45210. Reprinted by permission; Excerpts taken from the LECTIONARY FOR MASS/NEW AMERICAN BIBLE, copyright © 1970 by the Confraternity of Christian Doctrine, Washington, D.C., are used with permission. All rights reserved.

Table Of Contents

For Mom and Dad,
who lovingly started me
along the road
and first showed me
the signs to look for ...

Introduction

Lent is often described as a journey.

In the Scripture readings of the season, we travel with Jesus on his journey to Jerusalem where he completes his mission and ministry as Redeemer.

We wander in a 40-day "desert experience," beginning with the ashes that confront us with our sinfulness and ending in our own re-creation at Easter.

We climb some hard steps during Lent, facing the fact that we are less than the people we would like to be and profess to be.

The days of Lent and the Easter Triduum are special steps we travel in the pilgrimage of our lives. In any journey we look for road signs — markings, landmarks, and signals that indicate that we are traveling in the right direction, that the road we are on will lead us to our destination. This book is a collection of roadsigns for the Lenten journey. The "roadsigns" collected here have been found in the daily newspaper, in literature, in the theater, in everyone's memories of growing up, and even in the every day. Each "road sign" points to the reality of the themes of the Lenten Scriptures in our pilgrimage.

Roadsigns has been written especially with the homilist in mind. May these short reflections inspire creative and meaningful sharing around the Lord's table this Lent.

To those who might use this for personal reflection, for small group prayer and discussion, may this collection be the beginning of marking your own Roadsigns along the everyday road to Easter.

May we all meet at the end of our Lenten road in the peace and light of the Lord of the Easter promise!

ASH WEDNESDAY

FIRST READING: Joel 2:12-18
Rend your hearts, not your garments, and return to the LORD, your God.

SECOND READING: 2 Corinthians 5:20-6:2
... In him, we might become the very holiness of God.

GOSPEL: Matthew 6:1-6. 16-18
... Your Father who sees in secret will repay you.

Welcome to the Springtime

During the next few weeks, our world is going to change dramatically. The days will grow longer and warmer. The ice and snow will melt away and the first buds of spring will appear. The air will begin to feel a little more like summer and a little less like winter. The drab and darkness of winter will be transformed into the color and promise of spring.

Likewise, the symbols of ashes and purple and somberness that mark today's liturgy will be eclipsed in six weeks by the light and flowers and Alleluias of the Easter celebration.

The change we see *around* us should also be experienced *within* us during these weeks of Lent. In fact, the very word "lent" has come down to us from the ancient Anglo-Saxon word, "lencten," meaning "springtime." Unfortunately, we tend to look at Lent as something to be endured rather than to be observed ... a time of "not doing this" and "giving up that" ... a time to feel lousy so we can feel good on Easter Sunday. Sadly, we often view Lent as a time for *not* doing, for *avoiding*, instead of as a time for *doing*, for *becoming*.

Like springtime, Lent should be a time for transformation, for change, for becoming the people that God has called us to be. It is a time, as the prophet Joel tells us in the first reading, for "rending our hearts and not our garments."

The ashes we are about to receive should be quiet symbols of something much deeper, much more powerful, much more lasting that is taking place within us. In accepting these ashes we acknowledge the fact that we are sinners — that we are less than faithful to our baptismal name of Christian. But in accepting these ashes we also accept the challenge to become, as Paul writes to the Corinthians, "the very holiness of God."

*

Father, give us your peace during this Lenten season. May the days ahead be a time of quiet change within each one of us, that our hearts and spirits may be transformed from the winter of sin and despair into the spring of Easter hope and life in you.

THURSDAY

after Ash Wednesday

FIRST READING: **Deuteronomy 30:15-20**
I have set before you life and death, the blessing and the curse. Choose life, then, that you and your descendents may live, by loving the LORD, your God, heeding his voice and holding fast to him.

GOSPEL: **Luke 9:22-25**

Crossmarks

H. Ross Perot, the computer magnate and philanthropist, says that he learned the importance of charity and generosity from his mother.

Growing up during the Depression, young Ross saw that nobody in need would ever be turned away from the Perot house without a hot meal and whatever few cents could be scraped together. One day Ross began to notice that beggars would seldom stop at any of the other houses on the Perot's street, but the poor never failed to stop at the Perot's. All the other houses on the street belonged to families with the same means as the Perots; but the needy, it seemed, would make a beeline for the Perot house.

The boy soon discovered why: someone had scratched a chalk mark on the curb in front of their house. The mark was made by someone who had received help from Mrs. Perot. It was meant to be a sign to others that here was a house where they would be welcomed.

Ross reported to his mother what he had discovered and asked her if he should wash the chalk mark off the curb. His mother was emphatic, "Leave the mark exactly where it is. We should be honored by that chalk mark because it tells everyone that our house is a place of warmth and shelter."

The cross is not easy to take up. It represents a value system that often runs counter to our own. The choices it represents are sometimes the choices we would rather not opt for. This season of Lent calls us to take up the cross joyfully (as the Perot family joyfully "took up" the chalk mark on the curbside), instead of seeking ways to "erase" the cross from our lives.

*

Father, life presents us many choices, choices that are not easy to make. Help us to take up your Son's cross, choosing the life that it represents and the hope that it promises.

FRIDAY

after Ash Wednesday

FIRST READING: Isaiah 58:1-9

This ... is the fasting that I wish: sharing your bread, rather, with the hungry, sheltering the oppressed and homeless; clothing the naked when you see them, and not turning your back on your own. Then your light shall break forth like the dawn ....

GOSPEL: Matthew 9:14-15

How can the wedding guests go in mourning so long as the groom is with them?

A *"Giving"* Lent

Probably the biggest challenge that an advertising or public relations firm could take on would be to make Lent a time people actually looked forward to.

Lent is *nobody's* favorite time. When most of us were children, Lent was a real "downer." It meant giving things up and doing without. The watchword of Lent was self-denial. To keep a good Lent was measured in terms of the candy not consumed, the movies not seen, the cigarettes not smoked, the hamburgers not eaten.

Now, there is certainly still a place for "giving things up" during Lent, to remind ourselves that although God has given us so much, he has promised us even more.

But as today's readings point out, more important than giving things up during Lent is the idea of *giving* during Lent. Lent is time for conversion — for making our lives what the Lord intends for them to be. Such a conversion is an *active* process. To keep a good Lent, then, should be marked by active, positive experiences of giving, sharing and enriching.

*

Father, may this season of Lent be a worthy offering to you. Inspire us to fast from self-centeredness and greed, to put on the sackcloth of kindness and charity for others, to place upon our heads the ashes of mercy and compassion.

SATURDAY
after Ash Wednesday

FIRST READING: Isaiah 58:9-14

If you bestow your bread on the hungry and satisfy the afflicted; then light shall rise for you in the darkness, and the gloom shall become for you like midday.

GOSPEL: Luke 5:27-32

I have not come to invite the self-righteous to a change of heart, but sinners.

Not the "Upper Crust"

Jesus did not exactly hang around with what would be considered the "cream" of Jerusalem society.

Fishermen, laborers, shepherds, tax collectors, peasants, and even prostitutes made up the crowds who would gather to hear him teach; after all, it was exactly to these poor sinners that Jesus came to bring hope and salvation.

But, in reading the Gospels, one suspects that Jesus actually liked these people. Jesus saw something special in each of them — Matthew the despised tax collector, the Samaritan woman by the well, Peter the gruff fisherman. Jesus wanted them to be the best they could be and showed them the way to that end. But first, Jesus accepted them for what they were — very imperfect people.

And that's the great paradox of the Gospel: despite all the selfish and un-Christian things we do, God never stops loving and caring about us.

So if God chooses the likes of *us* to be his friends, can't we at least be friends to one another?

*

Father, help us to accept who we are and to realize our need for you. And give us the openness to accept others and the goodness that each person possesses that can, if we let it, bring us closer to you.

MONDAY
of the First Week of Lent

FIRST READING: Leviticus 19:1-2. 11-18
You shall love your neighbor as yourself.

GOSPEL: Matthew 25:31-46
"I assure you, as often as you did it for one of my least brothers, you did it for me."

The Nameless Poor

The old geezer in rags sleeping on a heating grate in a downtown alley....

The skeletal form of an African mother, hugging her hungry child, shielding her baby from the searing sun and the bugs, waiting for help that will never come....

The child looking for her family amid the rubble of wooden planks and tin sheeting that was their house before the earthquake struck....

The teenager trying just to survive in the jungle of the inner-city ghetto ... and the mother of that teenager, struggling through a series of dead-end jobs so that, perhaps some day, her children might escape the poverty she has always known....

The nameless poor. We see their pictures in newspapers

and magazines, we hear their stories on evening newscasts, we may have even met them ourselves at one time or another. But the poor whom we overlook or pass by are not nameless. They share a name that we know and recognize. Their name is Jesus. "Whatever you do for one of the least of my brothers and sisters, you have done for me. Whenever you neglect one of these least ones, you have neglected me."

*

Father, melt the cold indifference that can darken our vision. May we see in the face of the poor, the troubled, and the forgotten the face of him who is your Word and Light, Jesus the Christ.

TUESDAY

of the First Week of Lent

FIRST READING: Isaiah 55:10-11

Just as from the heavens the rain and snow come down ... making the earth fertile and fruitful, so shall my Word be that goes forth from my mouth.

GOSPEL: Matthew 6:7-15

In your prayer do not rattle on like pagans ... This is how you are to pray: "Our Father in heaven ... "

A Milkman's Prayer

One of the most delightful characters of the stage is Tevye the milkman in the musical *Fiddler on the Roof.* Life for poor Tevye is a constant series of problems, challenges and confrontations — from the marriages of his daughters to the expulsion of his family and neighbors from their Russian village. But through it all, Tevye maintains his faith in God's presence in his life and in the life of his people.

Perhaps the most beautiful thing about Tevye's character is his sense of prayer, his awareness of God's constant presence in every moment and in every event. He gathers with his family to begin the Sabbath ("May the Lord protect and defend you") and with his neighbors for the wedding of his eldest daughter ("Sunrise, Sunset").

As he delivers his milk, Tevye talks through his problems with God and asks God to help him to understand the Lord's purpose in the events that befall his family and friends: "Sometimes I think when things are too quiet up there, You say to Yourself: 'Let's see what kind of mischief I can play on my friend Tevye?'" Even Tevye's "showstopper" song, "If I Were a Rich Man," is a actually a prayer to the Lord.

For Tevye, prayer is not only rituals and formulas, but prayer is an awareness of God's constant presence, an attitude of openness to seeing God in the people and events around you. Tevye approaches prayer in much the same way that St. Teresa of Avila did: "Imagine the Lord himself at your side ... Stay with this good friend as long as you can."

*

Father, teach us not to confine our prayer to words and rituals. May every moment you give us be part of a continuous, life-long prayer of praise to you, you who are Giver and Nurturer of all life.

WEDNESDAY
of the First Week of Lent

FIRST READING: Jonah 3:1-10
The word of the LORD came to Jonah: "Set out for Nineveh, and announce to it the message I will tell you."

GOSPEL: Luke 11:29-32
For at the preaching of Jonah the Ninevites reformed, but you have a greater than Jonah here.

Jet Lag

A friend called not too long ago from the airport. He was passing through and just had a few minutes between flights to call to say hello. He had been traveling quite a bit and remarked how jet lag had completely thrown off his sense of time.

We really don't have to travel cross-country or overseas to have our sense of time thrown off. We can lose our perspective easily right here. It seems the people and things that are really important to us often get shuffled off to one side because of business or projects that always seem to demand our immediate attention.

(Consider, too: How many of us, before we even plan to make a telephone call just to say hello or to make a date to spend time with our families, have to check our calendar books first?)

Lent is a time to get things back into perspective, to refocus our attention and time on the people and things that we really care about and believe in, that give our lives joy and fulfillment.

*

Father, don't let us live our lives like we're living every day in airports. Don't let us be ruled by schedules and calendar books. May this Lenten season be a time for us to center our lives in you, you who are Lord of this age and the age to come.

THURSDAY
of the First Week of Lent

FIRST READING: Esther 12:14-16. 23-25

Queen Esther's prayer: "As a child I heard from the people of the land of my forefathers that you, O Lord, chose Israel from among all peoples and you fulfilled your promises to them. Save us by your power and help me, who am alone and have no one but you, O LORD."

GOSPEL: Matthew 7:7-12

If you, with all your sins, know how to give your children what is good, how much more will your heavenly Father give good things to anyone who asks him!

"Thank You, Lord, for Thunking Us Up. Amen."

Theodore Geisel, better known as the writer and illustrator of children's books, Dr. Seuss, received this letter from an eight-year-old:

"Dear Dr. Seuss, you sure thunk (sic) up a lot of funny books. You sure thunk up a million animals ... Who thunk you up, Dr. Seuss?"

That's a good question to consider every day, but especially during this Lenten season. "Who thunk us up?" Who gave us life and continues to breathe life into all of creation?

Who continually calls and welcomes us back, despite the many times and the many ways we reject him? Who is the source of all that is good and compassionate? Who "thunk" us up ... and keeps thinking about us ... and continues to love us?

Most of our prayers are "gimmee" prayers — gimmee strength, O Lord ... gimmee good health, O Lord ... gimmee a promotion or raise, O Lord.

Certainly petition to the Lord is a dimension of prayer. But in today's Gospel, Jesus points out that there is more to prayer than "gimmee." Prayer is not a gadget we use when nothing else works.

Note that Jesus does *not* say "Ask, and you will get what you ask for. Knock, and the door to the mansion of your dreams will be opened to you." He says, "Ask and you will receive. Knock, and it will be opened to you." What will you receive? What will be opened to you? Jesus explains it this way: "If you, with all your sins, know how to give your children what is good, how much more will your heavenly Father give good things to anyone who asks him!"

Begging the question? Not really. The point is that every person has received a great deal from God — whether we realize it or not. True men and women of prayer are aware of God's presence and gifts in their lives and trust in the Lord's providence in whatever their lives hold for them.

Prayer, then, should be, first and foremost, an attitude of trust and acceptance of God's presence in our lives. An attitude of prayer is not occasional but constant, on-going; it is not just asking God for something that is not, but it is thanking him for what is and for what has been; it speaks not only in the rituals of public worship, but it speaks in the silence of the heart. Queen Esther's "prayer" in the first reading today is a beautiful example of prayer that reflects this kind of attitude: openness, acceptance, trust and thanksgiving, as well as petition.

*

Father, may every moment of our lives be a prayer to you. May every word we utter, every task we undertake, and every thought we consider express an attitude of thanks for all you have given us, and of trust in all you have promised us.

FRIDAY
of the First Week of Lent

FIRST READING: Ezekiel 18:21-28

Do I indeed derive any pleasure from the death of the wicked? says the LORD God. Do I not rather rejoice when the wicked turns away from his evil way that he may live? Is it my way that is unfair, or rather, are not your ways unfair?

GOSPEL: Matthew 5:20-26

If you bring your gift to the altar and you recall your brother has anything against you, ... go first and be reconciled with your brother, and then come and offer your gift.

A Visit to Hell

The Oscar-winning movie, *Platoon*, is the brutally realistic story of a group of soldiers fighting in Vietnam. The film was written and directed by Oscar Stone, a Vietnam veteran. The story is told through the eyes of Chris Taylor, a 21-year-old child of privilege who volunteered for the draft and Vietnam because he was convinced that young men who had grown up with less than him could teach him something about life.

At one point, after taking some casualties on patrol, Chris' platoon enters a village and begins to seek its revenge.

The young volunteer, stunned and outraged by the death of his comrades, begins to take part in the brutality, but then becomes horrified by it. At the end of his tour of duty, Chris is wounded. As he is airlifted to safety and medical care, we hear Chris' voice speaking in the present, remembering the scene we have just watched:

"Those of us who did make it have an obligation to build again, to teach others what we know and to try with what's left of our lives to find a goodness and a meaning in this life."

Chris has learned a great deal from his Vietnam experience, but not what he expected. He writes to his grandmother from 'Nam, "I have been to hell, Grandma. Hell is a place where there is no reason."

The readings today challenge us to look at our value system. We often approach the world from an eye-for-an-eye, us-versus-them, bottom-line mentality. We're the good guys in the white hats and they're the bad guys in black hats.

But that kind of value system is not God's way. Retribution, no matter how warranted we think it might be, is not what Christ calls us to seek. To follow God's way means to rejoice in the return of those who have been lost to sin; to be Christ's followers means to be a people of reconciliation, of forgiveness. To seek otherwise is the kind of destructive insanity that is absolute hell.

*

Father, help us to throw away the scales and rulers that cause us to seek angry retribution and to rejoice in the evil that befalls those who wrong us. Give us the courage and vision to remake our world from a hateful hell into your kingdom of love and concern.

SATURDAY
of the First Week of Lent

FIRST READING: Deuteronomy 26:16-19

Today you are making this agreement with the LORD: he is to be your God and you are to walk in his ways and observe his statutes, commandments and decrees, and to hearken to his voice.

GOSPEL; Matthew 5:43-48

My command to you is: love your enemies, pray for your persecutors. If you love those who love you, what merit is there in that? You must be perfected as your heavenly Father is perfect.

Looking Glass

Two little brothers were having a terrible fight. But rather than punish or spank them, their wise mother called the boys outside and asked them to clean a grimey glass table top that had been stored in the garage all winter.

The two boys took positions on opposite sides of the glass and began scrubbing off the dirt with paper towels and glass cleaner. As the grime disappeared, the two boys had no choice but to see each other's reflections in the glass. Angry scowls soon turned to smiles and laughter.

Lent is the season of reconciliation, of wiping away the hate and prejudice that dirty our world. It is a time for tearing down walls and building bridges to those, frankly, we've become much more comfortable and happier having nothing to do with.

In the Greek, the word that we hear in today's Gospel as "love" is "agape" — the word indicates benevolence and good will, rather than the more emotional "love" as we usually understand love. The love or "agape" of today's Gospel is a matter of will rather than of emotion. The love that Christ teaches us to have for our enemies means that no matter how much we may be hurt by someone, we will never let bitterness close our hearts to that person nor will we seek anything but good for that "enemy." That can be very tough. But that is the way of the cross.

*

Father, help us to be people of "agape": to love the unlovable, to reach out to the alienated and to seek what is good for all people in all things.

MONDAY

of the Second Week of Lent

FIRST READING: Daniel 9:4-10

We have rebelled and departed from your commandments and your laws ... But yours, O LORD our God, are compassion and forgiveness!

GOSPEL: Luke 6:36-38

Be compassionate, as your Father is compassionate ... For the measure you measure with will be measured back to you.

The Numbers Game

From the moment we memorize the sequence of numbers from one to ten, we measure ourselves and many of our relationships by counting. Children count baseball cards and Matchbox cars. Athletes count every throw, every second, every point, every assist. Business people count billings, bookings, and the bottom line — even the miles flown on an airline are counted! Value is measured in terms of dollars and cents: We are "worth" x number of dollars, our homes are valued at x number of dollars. Even art is evaluated in numbers — the number of tickets sold, the weekly gross, the Nielson ratings, the price the painting brought at auction.

How do we measure success? Through the numbers:

through statistics, through the polling data, through profit and loss statements.

The person of faith, however, is called to invest love, caring, and compassion in people without looking for a profit. Just as God constantly calls us back to him when we reject him so many times and in so many ways, we Christians are called to look beyond numbers to see human beings as brothers and sisters and to seek the joy of serving them. God will make the "numbers work" in the end.

*

Father, open our eyes to look at the world with faith instead of sizing things up "by the numbers." May our love for others be limitless and unconditional, just as your love is for us.

TUESDAY
of the Second Week in Lent

FIRST READING: Isaiah 1:10. 16-20

Put away your misdeeds from before my eyes; ... Make justice your aim: redress the wronged, hear the orphan's plea, defend the widow. Come now, let us set things right ...

GOSPEL: Matthew 23:1-12

The greatest among you will be the one who serves the rest. Whoever exalts himself shall be humbled, but whoever humbles himself shall be exalted.

Playing Second Fiddle

Which instrument in a symphony orchestra do you think would be the most difficult to play?

The great conductor Leonard Bernstein was asked that question by a friend. The maestro thought for a moment, and then gave this surprising answer.

"Second fiddle," he said. "I can get plenty of first violinists. But to find one who can play second fiddle with enthusiasm — that's a problem. Yet, if there is no one to play second fiddle, we have no harmony."

Jesus' whole life is a parable of humble service to one's neighbors. For the person of faith, the question is not whether one has "star billing" or is relegated to playing "second fid-dle," but that he or she is able to give and contribute in the spirit of Christ.

*

Father, show us the joy of being your servant to others. May even our simplest acts of kindness help to create harmony from the discord around us. Give us ears to hear not just the notes we play but the harmony all of us can create together.

WEDNESDAY
of the Second Week of Lent

FIRST READING: Jeremiah 18:18-20

The people plot against the prophet: "Must good be repaid with evil that they should dig a pit to take my life?"

GOSPEL: Matthew 20:17-28

... the Son of Man has come, not to be served by others but to serve, to give his own life as a ransom for the many.

Greatness in Service

Mark Hatfield has been a United States Senator from Oregon since 1966. In his many years of public service — as a senator, as a governor, as Oregon's secretary of state, as a state representative and senator, and as a college professor and dean — Senator Hatfield has met and worked with many of the great leaders of the nation and the world.

Senator Hatfield once made this insightful observation:

"Some of the greatest people I have had the privilege of knowing not only are the most humble, but are those who express their humility by becoming actual servants in their relationships with others."

Senator Hatfield discovered in his own experience what Jesus teaches in today's Gospel: that greatness lies in service to others. And such service begins with seeing others as worthy of our efforts. This is the role and attitude of the "servant" that God asks us to assume in our lives. And, as his servants, he assures us that we can accomplish great things.

*

Father, inspire us with a sense of humility to realize that in serving others we serve you. By a new attitude of service, may we attain the greatness of life in you and with you.

THURSDAY
of the Second Week of Lent

FIRST READING: Jeremiah 17:5-10

Blessed is the man who trusts in the Lord, / whose hope is the Lord. / He is like a tree planted beside the waters / that stretch out its roots to the stream: / It fears not the heat when it comes, / its leaves stay green; / In the year of drought it shows no distress, / but still bears fruit.

GOSPEL: Luke 16:19-31

The parable of Lazarus and the rich man.

Reflection: Sharing the Blessings

Paul Newman is one of America's most popular and durable actors. He is known for his many superb films, including *Cat on a Hot Tin Roof, Butch Cassidy and the Sundance Kid, The Hustler, The Sting, Absence of Malice, The Verdict*, and his Oscar-winning performance as Fast Eddie Felson in *The Color of Money.*

But Paul Newman's name not only appears on theater marquees but also on supermarket shelves. In 1982, Newman, who loves to cook and is considered a superb chef, began to market his own line of foods, including salad dressing, spaghetti sauce and popcorn. The Newman companies have made almost $10 million in profits.

But all of the profits from the company, which Newman and a friend started on a whim, have all gone to charity. Newman's sauces and foods, for example, are building a special summer camp for children suffering from cancer and other diseases. When he announced the project, the actor said, "The wonderful thing about this project is the only limitation will be our own imagination."

Everyone knows that there is no sin in being rich. The moral question is how we use our wealth, whether we are rich in money, talent, education or any material or intellectual resources. In Christ's parable about Lazarus and the rich man, the rich man is condemned not because he is rich but because he fails to share his wealth with the poor at his own gate.

If we're willing to look, we'll find that there are many poor at our own gates. Some are begging for food, but others are begging for recognition, for compassion, and for understanding.

*

Father, give us the eyes of faith to see you in the poor and needy around us. May we give you thanks by giving in thanks for the many gifts you have given us.

FRIDAY
of the Second Week of Lent

FIRST READING: Genesis 37:3-4. 12-13. 17-28
Joseph's brothers, jealous of their father's love for him, sell him into slavery.

GOSPEL: Matthew 21:33-43, 45-46
The parable of the vineyard owner's son who is killed by jealous workers for his inheritance.

Destructive Jealousy

The central figure of the play/movie *Amadeus,* contrary to the title, is not the young Wolfgang Amadeus Mozart, but his rival, the composer Antonio Salieri. All of his life, Salieri only sought one thing — to be a composer. He had achieved a level of respect as court composer to Emperor Joseph II of Austria. But the discovery of the prodigy Mozart by the emperor threatens Salieri's world. Salieri rails against God:

"You gave me the desire to serve You — which most men do not have — then saw to it the service was shameful in the ears of the server. You gave me the desire to praise you — which most men do not feel — then made me mute ... Until this day I have pursued virtue with vigor ... I have worked the talent you allowed me. You know how hard I've worked! Solely that in the end...I might hear Your Voice! And now I hear it — and it says only one name: *Mozart!*"

Salieri then vows to block God by destroying the immature but gifted Mozart. Rather than encouraging and teaching the young composer, Salieri instead wages war against God for making him mediocre: for implanting in him a desire to serve as a composer and then making his service seem shameful in his own ears.

As the play continues, Salieri does destroy Mozart and he returns to his place of eminence among musicians. In the end, however, Salieri is condemned to "survive to see myself become extinct! Mozart's music sounded louder and louder through the world. And mine faded completely, til no one played it at all."

If someone else's success can inspire us to work harder to make our own lives better, that is good; but to seek only to diminish or destroy someone who has received or attained what we seek is nothing but senseless destruction.

The challenge of Lent is to rejoice in goodness wherever we find it — even if it deflates our fragile egos a little.

*

Father, help us not only to seek what is good, but to rejoice in what is good. May we recognize your hand in every blessing we receive — and may we give you thanks for the blessings you bestow on others. Let the goodness and success of others not threaten us, but inspire us to become worthy to be called your sons and daughters.

SATURDAY
of the Second Week of Lent

FIRST READING: Micah 7:14-15. 18-20
Who is there like you, the God who removes guilt and pardons sin ... Who does not persist in anger forever, but delights rather in clemency?

GOSPEL: Luke 15:1-3. 11-32
The parable of the prodigal son.

The Prodigal Son's Brother

Today's Gospel, the parable of the prodigal son, is one of the most widely known stories in all of Scripture.

The message is pretty straightforward: The father in the story is God, and the prodigal is anyone who falls away but returns and consequently is forgiven by God, our heavenly Father.

But let's consider for a moment the third major character in the story: the older son, who protests his father's welcoming back of his wastrel brother. Now admit it: Don't we sympathize with the older brother? Don't we understand his feelings? Don't most of us know someone who is constantly messing up his or her life and always has to be bailed out, usually by us? After awhile, you wonder if he or she really cares. The cries for help and forgiveness start to wear thin. We just want to say, "Enough! If you want to screw up your life, go ahead. Why should I care, if you don't?!"

And then, there are those people who use us, who do us in; but soon comes the moment when that person has "to pay the piper" (and maybe we've even "helped" to bring that encounter about). It's a wonderful moment, right?

That's when we are confronted with the second part of the prodigal son story, the parable of the prodigal son's brother. Christ calls us not to condemn or gloat or belittle the prodigals of life, but to rejoice in their return, to keep picking them up no matter how many times they fall, and to open our arms and welcome them back again and again and again.

*

Father, be with us on the road of this life. Just as you are there to pick us up when we stumble, may we be there to pick up and support those who stumble and fall. May we always remember that every one of us, at some time or another, is your prodigal son or daughter.

MONDAY
of the Third Week of Lent

FIRST READING: 2 Kings 5:1-15
The commander Naaman humbly washes in the River Jordan at Elisha's instruction and is cured of his leprosy.

GOSPEL: Luke 4:24-30
Like Elijah and Elisha, Jesus was not sent only to the Jews.

Prophets Among Us

In a rundown tenement in one of New York City's darkest ghettos, a small group of women begin their day long before dawn. Their day will be one of prayer and of caring for the homeless and hungry, the abandoned and the abused. They walk quietly through the city dressed in the simple Indian sari of Mother Teresa's Missionaries of Charity....

Despite the demands of their studies and jobs, a group of college students manage each week to spend a couple of hours being a friend to a youngster who has lost a parent. Most of these Big Brothers and Big Sisters say that they get as much out of those couple of hours as their little brothers and sisters do....

The cruel disease AIDS has claimed many lives. But

there are many beautiful stories of selfless volunteers who care for the sick throughout their painful ordeal. There are also many touching moments of reconciliation, of forgiveness, and of understanding between AIDS sufferers and their estranged families and friends....

All of these men and women are prophets. The word "prophet" comes from the Greek word meaning "one who proclaims." Not all prophets appear in the Old Testament — there are prophets among us right here and now who proclaim the word of God in their ministries, in their compassion and kindness to others, in their reaching out to tear down walls of misunderstanding and alienation.

*

Father, may our Lenten observance make us your worthy prophets. May every moment of our lives proclaim the Gospel of the Christ who has died, who has risen, and who will come again.

TUESDAY

of the Third Week in Lent

FIRST READING: Daniel 3:25. 34-43

Azariah's song to the Lord: " ... we follow you with our whole heart, we fear you and we pray to you. Do not let us be put to shame, but deal with us in your kindness and mercy."

GOSPEL: Matthew 18:21-35

The parable of the unforgiving steward: "My heavenly Father will treat you in exactly the same way unless each of you forgives his brother from his heart."

Pope John Paul's Lesson in Forgiveness

On the front page of *The New York Times* on December 28, 1983, appeared a photograph that is perhaps the most beautiful lesson in forgiveness ever taught. In the photo, Pope John Paul II is seen huddled in a corner of a jail cell, talking quietly with the man who had tried to kill him only three years before.

Following the meeting, the Pope told reporters: "The Lord has given me the grace to meet as brothers. All the events of our lives must confirm that God is our Father, and we are all his children in Jesus Christ and thus all are brothers."

The editors of *The Times* were moved to comment in

that day's editorial: "(Some may say,) 'Easy enough for the Pope to be forgiving; after all, he survived.' But it cannot have been easy for a man who nearly lost his life and suffered cruel wounds to face the man who had been so eager to inflict them. In meeting Mehmet Ali Agca to pardon his enemy, John Paul moved the world — and shamed the vengeful."

Our God is a God of mercy and forgiveness. Jesus revealed to us that God loves us like a father loves his less-than-perfect children, children who manage to get into varying degrees of trouble. The cutting edge of the Gospel is Christ's teaching on forgiveness: we must love and forgive each other as God loves and forgives us.

*

Father, give us the grace to meet all men and women as brothers and sisters. May the spirit of compassion and forgiveness that we embrace move our world — and shame the vengeful among us.

WEDNESDAY
of the Third Week of Lent

FIRST READING: Deuteronomy 4:1. 5-9
Moses speaks to the people of Israel: "... not to forget the things your own eyes have seen, nor let them slip from your memory as long as you live, but teach them to your children and your children's children."

GOSPEL: Matthew 5:17-19
Whoever fulfills and teaches these commands shall be great in the kingdom of God.

Touching the Future

Christa McAuliffe lost her life in the January 1986 explosion of the space shuttle Challenger. One of the things she took with her was a T-shirt a friend had given her. On the shirt was written, "I touch the future. I teach."

When she was chosen by NASA for the "Teacher in Space Program," Mrs. McAuliffe said, "I think the reason I went into teaching was because I wanted to make an impact on other people and to have that impact on myself. I think I learn sometimes as much from my students as they learn from me....

"Teachers don't put out fires or arrest people. We deal

with minds. All we can hand people at the end of the year is hope for the future. How do you translate that into dollars?"

In his biography of Christa McAuliffe, *Touch the Future*, Robert T. Hohler writes about the kind of teacher Mrs. McAuliffe was.

"In her second year of teaching in Washington, D.C., 80 percent of her students were black, poor, and culturally isolated. They had lived just outside Washington, a nerve center for international relations, but they knew nothing of the world beyond their backyards. Vowing to change that, she had contacted the Peace Corps and committed (her class) to a fundraising drive for a new school in Africa. They had raffled a television, held bake sales, a car wash and a talent show, and had raised enough money to build a one-room cinder-block school in a rural region of Liberia where there had been no school. (Mrs. McAuliffe's students) had learned about geography, international relations, community activity and, four years before Alex Haley's book, they learned about roots."

That kind of dedication to teaching is what today's readings ask of us: to be teachers of God's word to our children, friends, and associates through our commitment to what is right ... through our sense of compassion and caring in our dealings with others ... through our ethical and moral approach to business in the marketplace ... through our sense of awareness of and gratitude for all that God has done for us.

*

Father, you have given us the gift of a great teacher, Jesus Christ, who has taught us the way to you. May we be teachers of your Word to others, that all may learn of your goodness through our joy, our caring and our commitment to all that is good.

THURSDAY
of the Third Week of Lent

FIRST READING: Jeremiah 7:23-28

Listen to my voice; then I will be your God and you will be my people. Walk in all the ways that I command you, so that you may prosper.

GOSPEL: Luke 11:14-23

The man who is not with me is against me. The man who does not gather with me scatters.

"Let Me Get Back to You on That ... "

It's been said that one should never discuss religion or politics in polite company.

But this has happened to all of us:

You're at a party or reception making small talk and someone comes up to you and, in the course of the conversation, that person asks, "What do you think about such-and-such?"

You don't want to get into an intense conversation about this controversial topic, so you try to make a little joke or attempt to change the subject.

But your questioner will not be put off. "No, seriously, what do you really think about such-and-such?"

You then might offer something noncommittal like,

"Well, there are a lot of people who think that ... "

But your questioner challenges you, "Yes, but what do *you* think about such-and-such?"

At that point you may hastily look at your watch and say something like, "Oh my! Look at the time! Gee, I'd like to continue this but I really have to be going"; or, "Oh, there's so-and-so. We've been trying to get together for weeks. Will you excuse me?" and you make a quick exit.

Today's readings — especially those last two lines of the Gospel — challenge us to take a stand. As Harry Truman said, there comes a time when every individual has to say what he or she really believes. We who call ourselves Christians have to translate our beliefs into action. At some point in our lives, we have to decide: Are we with Christ, or against him? There are no gray areas, no "extenuating circumstances," no cop-outs. Are we with him, or against him?

*

Father, give us the courage to say "yes" to your Son's invitation to be your people. Open our hearts and minds to his word in every moment. With him, may we gather the treasures of your heavenly kingdom.

FRIDAY
of the Third Week of Lent

FIRST READING: Hosea 14:2-10
We shall say no more, 'Our god,' to the work of our hands ....

GOSPEL: Mark 12:28-34
The Lord our God is Lord alone! Therefore you shall love the Lord your God with all your heart, with all your soul, with all your mind and with all your strength.

Those Strange Gods of Ours

Remember when you were first taught the Ten Commandments?

Your teacher no doubt explained to you what each one meant (probably not going into great detail about the sixth and ninth commandments, leaving those two until you were a little older). As you learned them and memorized each one, you probably recalled all those times when you did not keep them: the times when you swore, when you missed Mass on Sundays, when you did not do as your parents told you, when you got into a fight, when you did not tell the truth. Everyone has experienced the "downside" of most of the commandments.

Except one. There was one commandment that everybody was safe on — the first commandment: "I am the Lord your God. You shall not have strange gods before me."

Hey, no problem. Nobody that I know worships statues or animals. There are no pagans in this neighborhood. God is number one with us, right? Sure, we might have our little lapses with the other commandments, but the first one? No problem.

But as we get older, sometimes we do place "strange gods" before the Lord — things that become the object of our lives: money, fame, prestige, security, comfort. We live our lives not in the service of God but in the service of money.

The Irish have a proverb: "Money swore an oath that no one who did not love it should have it."

*

Father, you are the source and center of our lives. May we never replace you with idols and other "gods." Help us to recognize and welcome you in everyone and in everything that is good.

SATURDAY
of the Third Week of Lent

FIRST READING: Hosea 6:1-6
For it is love that I desire, not sacrifice, and knowledge of God rather than holocausts.

GOSPEL: Luke 18:9-14
The parable of the Pharisee and the tax collector.

From the Stanley Cup to Hell and Back

In the 1970s, Derek Sanderson was one of the premier defense men in the National Hockey League, playing with the Boston Bruins. Less than a decade later, Sanderson — once one of the highest paid players in professional hockey — was sleeping on a bench in New York's Central Park, homeless and penniless, helplessly addicted to alcohol and drugs.

Sanderson remembers:

"One day I found myself fighting with a drunk over a half-empty bottle of whiskey that had been thrown in a garbage can. I thought, hey, I'm a former Boston Bruin, a star hockey player, and this guy is just a drunk. I looked at this guy right in the eye. And then it hit me: Wait a minute, I'm a drunk too. The cheering, the trophies, the N.H.L. record book didn't make me any better than this other guy. I was a drunk, too. Period."

Then and only then, Sanderson says, he could begin to deal with his problem.

The parable in today's Gospel calls us to embrace the humility of the tax collector and dispel the self-righteousness of the Pharisee. The experience of Derek Sanderson illustrates how destructive pride can be at its worst and how the humble acceptance of our own sinfulness can be the beginning of healing and reconciliation.

*

Lord, Jesus taught us to call you Father and to call each other brother and sister. Help us to realize that we are members of one human family. May we embrace humility that heals and the simplicity of the Gospel that rejoices in you as Father of us all.

MONDAY
of the Fourth Week of Lent

FIRST READING: Isaiah 65:17-21

Lo, I am about to create new heavens and a new earth ... For I create Jerusalem to be a joy and its people to be a delight; I will rejoice in Jerusalem and exult in my people.

GOSPEL: John 4:43-54

The official put his trust in the word Jesus spoke to him, and he started for home. The fever left the man's son at the very hour Jesus told him, "Your son is going to live."

Nobody's Child

Marie Balter was born in the winter of 1931 to a penniless alcoholic woman who gave her up for adoption at birth. She lived in a number of foster homes until the little six-year-old was adopted by an elderly and austere Italian couple. They disciplined her for offenses they only imagined by locking her out of their home, imprisoning her in the basement, and sometimes even tying her to a post. Marie finally fled their cruelty and eventually ended up committed to a mental hospital. When Marie was 18, her natural mother located her and signed her out of the hospital. But unable to deal with her mother's addiction to alcohol and drugs, Marie returned to the hospital voluntarily.

For the next 20 years, Marie barely existed in the mental hospital. Doctors, in effect, "wrote her off" as a hopeless schizophrenic. She was treated with massive doses of back tranquilizers, ice baths, and drugs. She attempted suicide several times.

But a compassionate doctor discovered that Marie's condition was misdiagnosed. Marie actually suffered from depression and panic disorder, which includes muscle spasms, contractions of the hands and feet, choking, hyperventilation, and hallucinations. With the proper care, Marie was eventually weaned from her strong medication and resolved to deal with her extreme depression and panic disorder.

Marie recovered well enough to continue her rehabilitation in the home of a volunteer married couple. Through her own resolve and with the help of a great many people who cared, she learned to live on her own and even went to college. Marie eventually married and went on to earn her master's degree at Harvard. Life was still hard — she had to cope with the sudden death of her husband at the age of 45 and her own bout with cancer. But she coped, she says, because "people loved me and taught me how to love."

Seventeen years after leaving, Marie returned to the menatal hospital — not as a patient but as a member of the counseling staff. Today, Marie Balter is the respected administrator of her own institute for the treatment, training, and research for psychiatric and mental illness.

(Marie Balter's story was the subject of the award-winning CBS TV movie *Nobody's Child*.)

Marie Balter's life shows how love and compassion can be agents for healing and bringing forth life. Hers is a story of resurrection.

There are so many people who are awaiting resurrection — to rise from despair, cynicism, and alienation to a life filled with joy, hope, and a sense of belonging. Such is the resurrection and healing that we can bring to our world.

As Marie Balter tells audiences today, "We are destroying ourselves by the things we don't do, the respect and love we don't show to one another."

*

Father, you give us so many opportunities to heal divisions and to bring others up from despair to joyful fulfillment. Give us the patience, wisdom, and courage to bring resurrection and healing to our broken world.

TUESDAY
of the Fourth Week of Lent

FIRST READING: Ezechial 47:1-9. 12

I saw water flowing out from beneath the threshold of the temple ... Wherever the river flows, every sort of living creature that can multiply shall live ... Along both banks of the river, fruit trees of every kind shall grow.

GOSPEL: John 5:1-3. 5-16

Jesus cures the sick man by the Sheep Pool called Bethesda.

The Resurrection Plant

In the desert regions of America and the Near East, there is a plant that has the extraordinary ability to come to life after appearing to be dead.

The plant is called, not surprisingly, the "resurrection plant." In the presence of water, a resurrection plant will flourish with green, fern-like leaves. But when moisture is scarce, a resurrection plant, unlike most plants that have to wait for water to come to them, will uproot itself and wither into a dry, ball-like mass of apparently dead matter. The wind blows it across the desert, even for years, until water is found. Once water is found or after rain, the resurrection plant sinks its roots into the wet ground and springs to life once again.

In our travels through this life, we are like resurrection plants. We are life-less until we discover meaning and purpose. When we have found the life-giving water given by Christ, we grow and flourish in his spirit of love, compassion, and community.

*

Father, may this Lenten season be a time for renewing and re-creating our lives. May the waters that first purified us at baptism continue to flow within us and through us, to bring the healing presence of Christ to our hurting world.

WEDNESDAY
of the Fourth Week of Lent

FIRST READING: Isaiah 49: 8-15
In a time of favor I answer you, ... to restore the land and allot the desolate heritages ... I will cut a road through all my mountains, and make my highways level.

GOSPEL: John 5:17-30
Those who have done right shall rise to live; the evildoers shall rise to be damned.

The Ethics Doctor

Dr. Paul Mok is a psychologist who has worked with large corporations directing employee seminars on values. His firm, Training Associates of Dallas, has worked with such companies as General Electric, IBM, Smith-Kline Beckman, and Exxon. Doctor Mok helps employees and senior executives who have difficulties in balancing the competitive demands of their jobs with ethical concerns.

He says that many executives find that their expectations of ethical behavior are overridden by the pressure to cut costs, gain new business, and increase profits.

"Many people over time become desensitized to their own values and accept what goes on around them as 'the way things are.' People have to decide what they can live with and what they can't. Our studies show that only about one in four adults in the United States instinctively would be honest, rule-following and conforming. That leaves a lot of the rest of us who may cheat, abuse company resources or violate ethics and then justify it on the grounds that we're not paid enough or the rules are idiotic.

"It is not enough to have people sign or read an ethics statement once a year. If you don't spend some time in a company on ethics, if you don't verbalize it and have dialogue among middle managers and their subordinates, then ethics will take a remote back seat in people's consciousness."

Not only do the pressures of our result-oriented world make us shelve our values and sense of ethics, but the systems we have built even encourage us to do so, all in the name of good business and competition.

Lent calls us to re-create our world, to remake our lives into what we want them to be, to "restore the land and allot the desolate heritages ... to cut through all the mountains, and make my highways level," as Isaiah writes in today's first reading.

We have heard God's Word in the voice of Christ. We have to make the conscious decision to let that Word live in every dmension of our lives.

*

Father, open our minds and hearts to the Word of your Son. Help us to live that Word not only in church, but in our homes, our classrooms, our work places and meeting places.

THURSDAY
of the Fourth Week of Lent

READING: Exodus 32:7-14
Moses pleads for the Israelites before the Lord.

GOSPEL: John 5:31-47
If you believed Moses you would believe me, for it was about me that he wrote. The Scriptures also testify on my behalf.

Messenger to Humankind

Elie Wiesel, winner of the 1986 Nobel Peace Prize, has kept alive, through his many books, articles, and lectures, the memory of those millions of Jews who perished in the Holocaust of World War II. Wiesel, whose parents and sister perished in the Nazi death camps, writes not to condemn the human race, but to remind the world of the preciousness of the humanity we all share.

The Nobel Committee called Elie Wiesel a "messenger to mankind." In an interview just before the presentation, Elie Wiesel talked about the responsibility of being a "messenger."

"The last week in Buchenwald ... the Americans were coming closer, so the Germans decided to evacuate the camp.

There were 80,000 in the camp and they were going to evacuate 10,000 every day. Most of those who left were killed, either on the way, or on the trains: starved or shot. To leave (the camp) meant death....

"By chance, I always happened to be the eleven thousandth (who remained behind). Sometimes I was 30 or 40 people away from the gate. The gate was open, people were going. But they would let out only 10,000, then they'd stop. And I'm very often haunted by the person who was the ten thousandth. Since I cannot bring him back, I must speak for him ... I choose to be his messenger because he, I hope, is now my messenger."

We who have encountered Christ in our lives are now his messengers to the world. We are called to be the messengers of the Risen Christ who is now our messenger and advocate in the kingdom of God to come.

*

Father, make us worthy messengers of Christ. May our compassion and charity give effective witness to the good news of his Resurrection.

FRIDAY
of the Fourth Week of Lent

FIRST READING: **Wisdom 2:1. 12-22**
The wicked will seek to destroy the just one who condemns them for their wickedness.

GOSPEL: **John 7:1-2. 10. 25-30**
I have not come of myself ... I was sent by One who has the right to send ... It is from him that I come.

Conquering Crosses

Jan Kemp was one college professor who would not "play the game." An instructor at the University of Georgia, she was fired because she refused to change the failing grades of six Georgia athletes. She sued the university over her dismissal. Her case revealed how education often takes a back seat to big-time college sports — how the system exploits college athletes by not demanding more from them in the classroom. Four long years later, Jan Kemp won her job back. More importantly, because of her challenge, the University of Georgia and many other schools have begun to make important reforms in their athletic programs....

Richard Pastorella was a member of the New York City Police Bomb Squad. On New Year's Eve 1982, he and his team were called to defuse a bomb that had been planted in a government building. Before they could finish their dangerous task, the bomb exploded. Detective Pastorella lost his vision and most of his hearing and suffered severe burns on his right hand and face. His career as a policeman was over. In struggling through his own painful convalescence, Richard and his wife, Mary, met many other police officers who were permanently disabled by injuries suffered in the line of duty. The Pastorellas formed "The Police Self-Support Group" to help police officers and their families cope with the physical and emotional pain caused by their injuries. The support group is now a full-time job for Richard Pastorella....

On the day her teenage daughter was struck and killed by a drunk driver, Candace Lightner of California vowed to breathe meaning into her daughter's needless death. She founded MADD:Mothers Against Drunk Driving. The organization has increased public awareness about drunk driving and has been instrumental in the enactment of tougher penalties for drunk drivers around the country....

Jan Kemp, Richard Pastorella, and Candace Lightner all triumphed over the "wicked" (first reading), replacing injustice with justice and compassion. They have brought light and vision to darkness and misunderstanding. They have overcome the crosses in their lives and have brought new life to their communities. The season of Lent challenges us to bring forth life from the injustices, pain, and misfortunes that befall us.

*

Father, your Son triumphed over death on the cross to rise to new life in you. As he did, may we bring forth light and life from our own crosses.

SATURDAY

of the Fourth Week of Lent

FIRST READING: Jeremiah 12:18-20
But, you, O LORD of hosts, O just Judge, searcher of
mind and heart, ... to you I have entrusted my cause!

GOSPEL: John 7:40-53
The people and the Sanhedrin are divided over what to
make of this Jesus.

But Is It Art?

Most of us, especially as children, have played with a
paint-by-numbers set. Didn't we feel like real artists, with our
brushes and palette of paints and maybe even an easel to prop
up our "canvas" with the almost invisible blue outlines and
numbers? All we had to do was apply (never mind the many
effects that can be created by different kinds of brush strokes)
the numbered paint to the corresponding area of the picture.
Just stay between the lines and soon — *viola!* Instant art!

But we all know that paint-by-numbers is not true art.
Art has to be felt within the artist. Whatever the medium —
painting, sculpture, literature — art is the expression of that
something within the artist. The French writer Albert Camus
said that "every artist preserves deep within him a single

source from where, throughout his lifetime, the artist draws what he is and what he says, and when the source dries up, he withers and dies."

We sometimes approach our faith as a paint-by-numbers exercise. We see religion as a series of practices and rituals; to be "religious" means performing these rites in a careful and exact manner, as prescribed by custom or law. But faith is something that comes from within us: the Spirit of God dwelling in our hearts. That is the kind of faith that Jesus is asking of Israel and of us. He is calling us to more than just following the letter of the Law; he is calling us to internal conversion, to embrace the spirit of compassion and love that is central to the Law of the teachings of the prophets.

*

Father, may these days of Lent be a time of re-creation and conversion for us. May our faith become more than just a Saturday evening or Sunday morning routine, but a living, constant awareness of your presence in every facet and moment of our lives.

MONDAY
of the Fifth Week of Lent

FIRST READING: Daniel 13:1-9. 15-17. 19-30. 33-62
The two wicked judges falsely accuse Susanna of adultery but Daniel catches them in their lie.

GOSPEL: Years A and B: John 8:1-11
Let the man among you who has no sin be the first to cast a stone at her.

Year C: John 8:12-20
You pass judgment according to appearances, but I pass judgement on no man.

Project Rachel

The Church's teaching on abortion is certainly no secret. But what is not so well known is what the church communities in Milwaukee, Boston, and several other areas are doing to reach out to women and families who have experienced abortions.

Abortion is one of the most traumatic experiences a person can undergo. Both before and after the procedure, feelings of fear, anxiety, guilt, and panic are common — not only for the woman who has had the abortion, but also for the father of the unborn child, the grandparents, close friends, even medical personnel. For Catholics, the pain of abortion is intensified by a sense of alienation from God and Church.

So a group of priests in the Milwaukee area started a program they named "Project Rachel," after the Old Testament figure who wept uncontrollably over the loss of her child. Under the Project Rachel program, priests are given special training to counsel, to refer, and to minister the Sacrament of Reconciliation to women who have had an abortion. Counseling is also made available to parents, husbands, and friends who may have encouraged or supported a woman's decision to have an abortion. Some of the women who have come to Project Rachel have had abortions as long as 10 and 15 years before; many have had private counseling.

One organizer of Project Rachel explained, "Project Rachel reaches out to women who are suffering from remorse, guilt, depression, or spiritual alienation due to abortion. Project Rachel does not contradict or soften the Church's position on abortion. But the Church is also a loving and forgiving Church that must be present with the mercy of God for the women who have been carrying this burden all these years."

Sin is a reality in our world and we, as Christians, are called to reject all that is sinful. But we are called not to be a people of condemnation and judgment, but to be a people of reconciliation, reaching out to sinners who are just like us in the eyes of God. Like the dedicated people involved in programs like Project Rachel, we Christians are called to share the love and mercy of God instead of casting stones.

*

Father of forgiveness, make us a people of compassion. Give us the grace and the courage to reach out to those who fall along the road we all travel. Through our love for one another, may we may transform evil into good and darkness into light.

TUESDAY
of the Fifth Week of Lent

FIRST READING: Numbers 21:4-9
The people complained against God and against Moses,
their patience worn out by the journey.

GOSPEL: John 8:21-30
You belong to what is below; I belong to what is above.
You belong to this world — a world which cannot hold me.

Heading Home

In October 1983, Paul Tsongas was completing his first
term as the junior senator from Massachusetts. The 42-year-
old senator, who had distinguished himself as a senator and as
a leader of the Democratic party, was considered a rising star
on the national political scene.

But the discovery of lymphoma, a form of cancer,
changed all of that. Coming to grips with his illness, Tsongas
decided to leave the U.S. Senate in order to devote more of
his time and energy to being a husband and father to his three
young daughters. He tells the story of his illness and the decision to leave Washington in his book *Heading Home*.

"If all of a sudden I had the power to change history and prevent that original cell from undergoing its aberrational mutation, would I do it? Of course.

"But Isay that with hesitation.

"My illness made me face up to the fact that I will die some day. It made me think about looking back without regret. It made me appreciate (my wife) Niki's strength ... (It) caused me to realize the preciousness of the moments of (my children's) development.

"Life is a search for balance. We have to bring the scales back to balance.

"These changes, or more accurately reinforcements, are a precious gift. I will curse myself if I ever forget, if I ever take my present health for granted, if I ever let a day pass when I don't feel gratitude that it has been given to me."

Paul Tsongas confronted the preciousness and brevity of life. His illness led him to reorder the priorities and values in his life. Today's Gospel reading challenges us to do the same: to center our lives on "what is above," what is of God.

As Rabbi Harold S. Kushner writes in *When All You've Ever Wanted Isn't Enough*, "Our souls are not hungry for fame, comfort, wealth or power. Those rewards create almost as many problems as they solve. Our souls are hungry for meaning, for the sense that we have figured out how to love so that our lives matter."

*

Father, may our joys and hopes not be focused on financial success, power, or comfort. Help us to refocus our vision on seeking you in the love we share with all who call you Father.

WEDNESDAY
of the Fifth Week of Lent

FIRST READING: Daniel 3:14-20. 91-92. 95
God sends his angel to save Shadrach, Meshach, and Abednego from Nebuchadnezzar's furnace.

GOSPEL: John 8:31-42
If you live according to my teaching, you are truly my disciples; then you will know the truth, and the truth will set you free.

The Last Question

The greatest computer that had ever been designed was ready. Far more complex and sophisticated than anything that had been constructed before, this new computer was capable of solving the most intricate problems that, until then, defied analysis.

Scientists from all over the world gathered to be present at its unveiling. But they could not decide on what question to ask the computer to initiate its operations. While the scientists argued over intricate geometric functions, stress analysis, and the price of wheat, a janitor pushed himself forward through the crowd of academics. Still holding his broom, he typed onto the computer's keyboard, "Is there a God?"

A deathly silence fell over the control room, as all watched for the result. Slowly, the vast machine began to whirl and buzz into action. Lights flashed and a solemn buzz was heard from deep inside the machine. Slowly, a piece of computer paper emerged from the machine.

It read, "*Now* there is."

In searching for God, we sometimes imagine seeing him where he is not, when we make some *thing* the object of our lives. Technology, power, pleasure, money — these become the "golden statues" of our lives.

Christ has revealed to us the God who does not call us to be slaves, but instead calls us to love him like a Father and to love each other as brothers and sisters. The awareness of God as Father of all should be a liberating experience; it should free us from the enslaving conventions of materialism, of bigotry, of alienation.

*

Father, help us to shift our vision away from where you are not to where you are. May we see you in the faces of all people and serve you in reaching out to those we love, those in need, those who suffer, those who do not know you.

THURSDAY
of the Fifth Week of Lent

FIRST READING: Genesis 17:3-9
The Lord makes his covenant with Abraham, who will be "the father of many nations."

GOSPEL: John 8:51-59
Your father Abraham rejoiced that he might see my day.

Reflection: Tom Dooley's Legacy

In the 1950s, a young Catholic Navy doctor captured the imagination of America as he brought medical care to thousands of refugees in Asia. More than 25 years after his death, Dr. Tom Dooley's legacy lives on in many ways — and in many people.

Tom Dooley's legacy lives on, for example, in Dr. Wayne McKinney. When he first met Tom Dooley, McKinney was a New York public relations man who volunteered to help Dooley raise money for his work. The PR man soon joined the doctor in Indochina and became a hospital builder and administrator extraordinare: scrounging for hospital supplies and equipment and untangling the miles of government red tape to get supplies delivered and facilities built. But McKinney decided that what was really needed by these refugees was not more PR types or administrators but more doctors. So he returned to the United States and earned his medical degree.

Doctor McKinney returned to Indochina, where he worked until the fall of Saigon. Today, he treats Laotian, Cambodian, and Vietnamese children in Honolulu. "I can take care of (these children) because Tom Dooley planted a seed in my life," Doctor McKinney says today.

Tom Dooley's legacy also lives on in Betty Tisdale. She first volunteered her secretarial skills to help Doctor Dooley answer the thousands of letters he received. Soon Betty was spending her two weeks' vacation in Saigon each year working at the An Lac orphanage; during the rest of the year, she raised money and supplies for the orphanage. She and her husband have also adopted five Vietnamese girls and continue to work on behalf of a hospital serving the hill tribes in Thailand. "Until I met Tom Dooley," she says, "I never felt I was contributing much to others."

Tom Dooley has inspired so many people that the work he began lives on more than 25 years after his death. Today's readings speak to us of the legacy of the Old Testament covenant the Lord made with Abraham and how that legacy has been passed on to the people of the New Testament — us. The God who revealed himself to Abraham, the God whom Jesus revealed as our Father, continues to call us to be his people in this life with the promise of life in the next. As we approach the celebration of the perfection of this new covenant in the Passion, Death, and Resurrection of Jesus, let us pray that we might truly be his people.

*

Father, you have fulfilled your promise to us, first made to Abraham and fulfilled in the Risen Christ. From generation to generation, you have blessed us and cared for us, despite our rejection and ignorance of you. Give us the courage and insight to fulfill our promise to you — to be your people, a light for all nations.

FRIDAY
of the Fifth Week of Lent

FIRST READING: Jeremiah 20:10-13
For the Lord has rescued the life of the poor from the power of the wicked!

GOSPEL: John 10:31-42
" ... when, as he whom the Father consecrated / and sent into the world, / ... If I do not perform my Father's works, / put no faith in me. / ... Put faith in these works, / so as to realize what it means / that the Father is in me / and I in him."

"I Have No Hands But Yours ... "

During a bombing raid, a French village lost a beloved statue of Christ. The villagers painstakingly sifted through the rubble and managed to rebuild the statue, except for its hands. They searched and searched, but the pieces were never found. Finally, the villagers placed a plaque on the statue with the inscription: "I have no hands but yours."

"I have no hands but yours." That inscription beautifully summarizes one of the challenges of the Lenten season.

Scripture taught that those who were specially commissioned to some task by God were gods themselves. In today's Gospel, Jesus is specifically referring to Psalm 82:6. That psalm is a warning to unjust judges to cease their unjust ways and defend the poor and innocent. The appeal concludes, "(The Lord) says, 'You are gods, sons of the Most High, all of you.'"

Confronted by the Jews, Jesus says that he has been consecrated by God to perform the "many good deeds that I have shown you from the Father" — healing the sick, feeding the hungry, comforting the sorrowing.

We who have been consecrated by Christ in baptism take on the task of performing those same works. In caring for one another, in working for reconciliation among all people, in bringing the Gospel to our homes and work places, we "do the work" of Christ. We are the hands of Christ.

*

Father, may our hands be your hands. May your spirit inflame our minds and hearts that we may bring your life to our waiting world.

SATURDAY
of the Fifth Week of Lent

FIRST READING: Ezechiel 37:21-28
I will make of Israel one nation. My dwelling shall be with them. I will make with them a covenant of peace.

GOSPEL: John 11:45-57
Many of the Jews who had come to visit Mary, and had seen what Jesus did, put their faith in him. Some others, however, went to the Pharisees and reported what Jesus had done. "What are we to do," they said, " with this man performing all sorts of signs?"

2 + 2 = 4? *Depends* ...

A college was interviewing applicants for its presidency. The final three candidates were a mathematician, an economist, and a lawyer. The committee decided to conduct a final interview with each, and to ask each candidate the same question: "What is two plus two?"

The mathematician first pondered the question for some time, as mathematicians do. Then he said, "Speaking in real integers only, without logarithmic variables or square root factors, the answer is four."

Next the economist met with the committee: "Within standard statistical deviation, based on the expected Dow

Jones and AMEX averages, the answer, plus or minus one, is four."

Finally, the question was posed to the lawyer. He got up from the table, walked over to the windows and pulled down the shades. Then he made a dramatic turn toward the committee and asked, "How much do you want it to be?"

Amazing, isn't it, how people can witness the same experience or consider the exact same facts and come up with as many different conclusions, opinions, and interpretations as there are individual witnesses. And all of them absolutely correct! As John reports in today's Gospel, even Jesus' works and teachings were viewed very differently by different people — to many, he was the Messiah, but to the leaders of Israel, he was a threat that had to be eliminated.

The Gospel challenges us to recognize the prejudices, biases, and ambition that exist within each one of us and to understand how they affect the decisions we make. There is no room for irrational prejudices or self-serving ambition in the way the true follower of Christ deals with all the world offers. The Christian is called to approach the world honestly and courageously, to see the world and everyone and everything in it through the eyes of faith, in the spirit of the Gospel.

*

Father, open our minds and hearts to the light of faith. In every decision we make, in every action we take, may we bring your healing and peace to our families, our communities, and our world.

MONDAY
of Holy Week

FIRST READING: Isaiah 42:1-7

First song of the Servant of Yahweh: I, the LORD, ... formed you, and set you as a covenant of the people, a light for the nations, to open the eyes of the blind, to bring out prisoners from confinement.

GOSPEL: John 12:1-11

Mary anoints the feet of Jesus: "Let her keep it against the Day they prepare me for burial."

"Attitude Dancing"

The readings we will hear today, tomorrow, and Wednesday set the stage for the events of Thursday, Friday, and Saturday.

The Old Testament readings are from the prophet Isaiah; his selections are known as the songs of the Suffering Servant of Yahweh. In these passages, Isaiah writes about a Messiah who will *not* be the all-powerful liberator and conqueror that most people had hoped for and expected. The Messiah that Isaiah speaks of will be a healer and a teacher who will be rejected by those he has come to serve; but in the end, God will raise up this Servant as a light to all nations.

The events that lead up to Jesus' arrest are recalled in the Gospel readings we will hear: as Jesus prepares his followers for the fate that he knows awaits him, Judas Iscariot puts into motion his plan for Jesus' destruction.

Yesterday (Palm Sunday), we heard the story of the Passion of Jesus. Perhaps lost in the dramatic liturgy of Palm Sunday was yesterday's second reading, from Paul's letter to the Philippians. In that reading, Paul sets the theme for Holy Week quite clearly and succinctly: "Your attitude must be Christ's; he emptied himself ... he humbled himself to accept even death on the cross. God (has) highly exalted him and bestowed upon him the name above every other name."

Our attitude must be like Christ's. He does not stand on legalisms nor does he demand what is rightfully his. Despite his own suffering, humiliation, and rejection, Jesus reaches out to heal the confusion and hurt of those suffering with him. His is the attitude of the perfect Servant of God.

*

Father, as we begin this Holy Week and we remember and celebrate the Passion of Jesus, help us to embrace his attitude of compassion and love. May we become, like him, your servants by being servants to one another.

TUESDAY
of Holy Week

FIRST READING: Isaiah 49:1-6
Second song of the Servant of Yahweh: You are my servant, he said to me, Israel, through whom I show my glory ... I will make you a light to the nations, that my salvation may reach to the ends of the earth.

GOSPEL: John 12:21-33. 36-38
Jesus foretells how Judas and Peter will betray him.

Betrayal

The Passion of Jesus, as recounted in the Gospels, is a story of violence. When we read the Passion in the beauty of our churches, we can lose sight of what a violent, painful, and humiliating death Jesus suffered.

But, the physical pain Jesus endured notwithstanding, the saddest episode of all the events of Good Friday is Peter's denial of Jesus. At first, we wonder how Peter could ever say he did not even know Jesus, after all the fisherman had witnessed: the joy his teachings inspired, his healing of the sick, the raising of Lazarus from the tomb, the calming of the storm on the lake.

And yet, there is something inside of us that also says,

Peter, I understand. I understand the fear you felt. I understand the pressure you were under. I understand the how and why of your betrayal.

The word "betrayal" raises a great deal of indignation among us. We see "betrayal" as a sin of monumental proportions — the kiss of Judas and the treason of Benedict Arnold.

But we understand betrayal better than we are willing to admit. We betray others — and God — in so many small, non-monumental ways: betraying someone through mindless gossip, through aloofness, through silence.

*

Father, help us to realize the many ways we betray one another and you. May we be ready to give voice to the goodness of others and of you, you who are the Author of everything that is good.

WEDNESDAY
of Holy Week

FIRST READING: Isaiah 50:4-9
Third song of the servant of Yahweh: I gave my back to those who beat me, ... my face I did not shield ... The LORD God is my help.

GOSPEL: Matthew 26:14-25
Judas Iscariot plots with the chief priests to betray Jesus.

"Billy-Made-Me-Do-It"

Parents with two or more children understand the "Billy-made-me-do-it" syndrome. This condition manifests itself when a parent confronts one sibling with "Why did you finger paint the alphabet on the living room wall?" or "What possessed you to hang the cat from the chandelier?" The (allegedly) guilty child responds, "Billy made me do it."

Why did the perpetrator perpetrate the crime? Somebody else made me do it. I didn't want to. It wouldn't have been my choice, mind you, but it wasn't up to me. Billy made me do it.

Sound familiar? The funny thing is, though, the "Billy-made-me-do-it" syndrome is not just a childhood affliction. Many adults have been known to suffer from these same symptoms on occasion. We often call it "rationalizing."

In today's Gospel, we see a classic case of the "Billy-made-me-do-it" situation. Judas Iscariot probably reasoned: Look, this Jesus is going to get all of us killed, challenging and angering the Sanhedrin the way he does. Somebody has to to do something. And, hey, if I can make a little something in the process, so much the better. Survival made me betray him. Poverty made me betray him.

The chief priests, as we will hear, felt that they had to stop this Jesus character once and for all: He was teaching sacrilege and heresy. He was undermining the Jewish nation. And his teaching about love and freedom is the kind of rhetoric that could incite a riot among the people. We had to stop him or the Romans would have crushed us. The people made us do it. Our obligation and sense of duty made us do it.

But Judas will soon realize the seriousness of what he has done and pay the price. The reality of Christ's resurrection will shatter the rationalizations of the chief priests.

The Gospel challenges us to take responsibility for the choices we make and the values we embrace. We cannot let ambition or fear or the repercussions of associates stop us or limit us in responding to a situation with the unlimited love, compassion and generosity that Jesus demands of us. "Billy-made-me-do-it" and its many variations are not the responses of a person of faith.

*

Father, every day we are confronted with many problems, situations, and dilemmas that force us to make choices, tough choices. Give us the grace to respond to life's challenges as your sons and daughters and as brothers and sisters to one another.

HOLY THURSDAY:

Mass of the Lord's Supper

FIRST READING: Exodus 12:1-8, 11-14
The Lord instructs Moses on the observance of the Passover.

SECOND READING: 1 Corinthians 11:23-26
Every time, then, you eat this bread and drink this cup, you proclaim the death of the Lord until he comes!

GOSPEL: John 13:1-15
But if I washed your feet — I who am Teacher and Lord — then you must wash each other's feet.

The Parable Of The Mandatum

Tonight, the Rabbi who taught in parables teaches what is perhaps his most touching and dramatic parable.

Jesus and his closest friends have gathered together to celebrate their people's ancient festival of Passover. In the middle of the meal, Jesus — the revered Teacher, the Worker of miracles and wonders, the Rabbi the crowds wanted to make a king just a few days before — suddenly rises from his place as presider, removes his robe, wraps a towel around his waist and — like the lowliest of slaves — begins to wash the feet of the Twelve.

We can sense the shock that must have shot throughout that room. But, quietly, Jesus goes about the task, first one disciple, then the next, and so on. Jesus on his knees, washing the dirt and dust off the feet of the fisherman, then the tax collector, and so on. Despite Peter's embarrassment and inability to understand what is happening, Jesus continues the humiliating and degrading task.

When he is finished, Jesus explains his "parable": "What I just did was to give you an example: As I have done, so you must do."

The Teacher, who revealed the wonders of God in stories about mustard seeds, fishing nets, and ungrateful children, this last night of his life — as we know life — leaves his small band of disciples his most beautiful parable.

"As I, your Teacher and Lord, have done for you, so you must do for one another. As I have washed your feet like a slave, so you must wash the feet of each other and serve one another. As I have loved you without limit or condition, so you must love one another without limit or condition. As I am about to suffer and die for you, so you must suffer and, if necessary, die for one another."

Tonight should humble us. Tonight should make us uncomfortable. But tonight should enlighten us as to what it means to be a disciple of Jesus, to gather around his table and share his Eucharist with one another.

Tonight's parable is so simple, but its lesson is so central to what being a real Christian is all about. But it is Christ's most difficult parable to grasp.

*

Father, this evening we remember that night of the second Passover, the Passover of Jesus the Christ. In this Eucharist, we proclaim his life, his death, and the new life of his resurrection. In our service to one another, may we bring his Eucharist to our broken world.

GOOD FRIDAY:
The Passion of the Lord

FIRST READING: Isaiah 52:13-53:12
Fourth song of the Servant of Yahweh: But He was pierced for our offenses, crushed for our sins, upon him was the chastisement that makes us whole, by his stripes we were healed.

SECOND READING: Hebrews 4:14-16. 5:7-9
Christ became the eternal salvation for all.

GOSPEL: John 18:1-19:42
The Passion of our Lord Jesus Christ.

Brokenness

Michaelangelo's touching sculpture of the Pieta: the grieving mother, Mary, holding the broken body of her son, who has just been taken down from the cross.

The broken body of Jesus — humiliated, betrayed, degraded, scourged, abused, slain — is the central image of today's liturgy. Today, Jesus teaches us through his own broken body.

As a Church, as a community of faith, we are the body of Christ. But we are a broken body. As Archbishop Rembert Weakland explained, "We are not perfect. The Church is a broken society. We live in a community of broken people. We minister as broken people to broken people."

The suffering, the alienated, the unaccepted, the rejected, the troubled, the confused — all are part of the body, the broken body, of Christ.

This is the day to reflect on the reality of pain and suffering. This is the day to realize that the source of brokenness in our world — sin — is also a reality.

But the "Goodness" of Good Friday teaches us that there are other realities. For us who believe, the broken body of the Pieta is forever transformed into the full and perfect life of the Risen Christ. In conquering life's injustices and difficulties, we are healed and made whole in the reality of the Resurrection.

*

Father, accept us in our brokenness and heal us in our afflictions. Give us the humility to be suffering servants to one another, so that we may share, as one family of humankind, the eternal life of your obedient and suffering Servant, Jesus the Christ.

THE EASTER VIGIL

EPISTLE: Romans 6:3-11

Through baptism into Christ's death we were buried with him, so that, just as Christ was raised from the dead by the glory of the Father, we too might live a new life.

GOSPEL: Year A: Matthew 28:1-10
Year B: Mark 16:1-8
Year C: Luke 24:1-12

Jesus, the Nazarene, whom they crucified, has been raised up!

All Things Are New

Tonight's liturgy is about "newness," about beginnings.

Spring has come. The warmth of the season invigorates us. The first signs of new life have bud forth. The first flowers of the season decorate our church.

We have been warmed by the heat of a new fire. We have illuminated this place with its light.

We have heard again the stories of how God constantly made our ancestors in the faith a new nation — always forgiving them, always saving them from calamity, always giving them the courage and vision to start over.

And now, we hear the extraordinary news about the empty tomb. Christ is risen! Death is no longer the end but the beginning. All of humankind has been re-created. As we heard in the Easter Exsultet tonight:

"Father, how boundless your merciful love!
To ransom a slave, you gave away your Son.
O happy fault! O necessary sin of Adam,
       Which gained for us so great a Redeemer!
Night truly blessed
       When heaven is wedded to earth
       and we are reconciled with God."

The empty tomb of Easter speaks to us of new life, new creation, new hope. It is the promise of everlasting life in God. It should inspire us to bring resurrection in *this* life of ours, to renew and re-create our relationships with one another.

As long as the lights of heaven shine, we can make things new. We can start over. Jesus, the Risen Christ, makes all things new.

*

Father, may Christ the Morning Star illuminate our lives with his light of peace. May the joy of this night give us the grace and hope to make all things new in our lives as we look forward to the new life of his Resurrection. May every moment of our lives sing the "Alleluia" of Christ's empty tomb.